Sally Purcell

Dark of Day

Anvil Press Poetry

in association with
Rex Collings

Published in 1977
by Anvil Press Poetry
69 King George Street London SE 10
Distributed by Rex Collings Ltd
85646 029 X

Printed in England by
Skelton's Press, Wellingborough

Anvil Press Poetry acknowledges
the financial assistance of
The Arts Council of Great Britain

to Alasdair

Acknowledgments

Acknowledgments are due to the editors of the following magazines in which some of these poems first appeared:

Isis, Mawakif, The Minnesota Review, The Oxford Poetry Magazine, Oxford Poetry Now and *Priapus.*

Contents

Frontispiece

Juventus falls asleep in May time
under a flowering tree in the garden of fables
& the book he was reading,
allegory woven of Grail or Rose,
falls from his hand as the dream begins.

'Through drifting cloud appears that other garden —
I know the carvings that posture & warn
on its walls, the old man seated at the gate
who interprets dreams and symbols I shall meet,
and at the maze's heart one central tree,
the Rose of this world's love
— or the Dry Tree of Redemption, bearing
Phoenix that knows no death.

'And I, Lancelot, old Adam,
hear hermits gloss
images of that sacrifice,
may long for the shrivelled tree
where God's blood flamed,
shall never unlearn the Rose.'

Ariadne

Within the glowing maze Ariadne stands;
a buried city forms her dance's pattern,
her labyrinth is founded on the ruined banks of Troy.

Out of the bittersweet air she leads him,
the king who dances through his fate
in Troy-game, the unchanging order.

His long-told story ripens to an end,
he passes through the final glaring splendour,
and the ancient threads are wound again,
                                    rewoven.

On a Cenotaph

. . . le cadavre adoré de Sapho, qui partit
Pour savoir si la mer est indulgente et bonne

The sea will weave its light into your long dream
where Orpheus' head gives oracle & prophecy,
borne here on a bitter wave,
& still in summer dawn you will hear
the roaring waters cry.
Hoping to unriddle
the folds of sea or mirror, their brilliant sterility,
withdrawn from the common sun you voyaged
out from the white headland,
following a dark winter's moon.

We stand in cold and ruins, for our spring will never
come.

After any Wreck

Here
we have come at last
to a place out of the wind —
we look down from the doorway
of a small stone hut,
peer through mist and drizzle
for the lost sunlit land

and know
that there the waves are gnawing polished beams,
night is fallen on bright columns,
and the sea-sifted weed
floats tranquil over golden tiles.

In this hard refuge
on a hill above Atlantis,
hear only how
a cry from the despairing sea
is broken on the wind.

Tristan

After the sea came the wilderness,
the forest of Broceliande —
one moment out of time on a charmed sea,
becalmed and shining between worlds, was enough
to enslave me thought and will,
to bring me to this coil & tangle.
Your ocean gives horizon, flat clarity, meaning,
and whorls each alone in his hollowness like a shell,
but leads into those thickets of the Wood
where form & horizon perish, where Iseult
becomes an outlaw's mate
and the queenly seat is empty.

I cannot sing to sunlit air,
but I carve my rune on the hazel bough
in this wood of Morrois that holds me.

Early Irish Picture

Along the edge of night
moves the saint who has chosen his path
      of rejection,
to be traveller & stranger wandering
beyond the glass-green rim of the sky
      to seek his kingdom.

Brandan has sailed for his golden Isle,
Columbanus taken this world for pilgrimage.

ii

From the sun's holy tree, oracular oak,
moves the servant of the moon,
      rejecting other images,
pursuing his white martyrdom,
the lunar design that is clear
      in its darkness.

He comes alone to a secret land,
between cold marsh & ruined garden.

Two Kinds of Magic

A clouded moon mask
looks into the wood
where a dead king flames brightly;
the sun has lapped his blood,
the crackling forest
feeds on him in darkness
— and lights flare pale among the Roman city's bones
where enchanters draw the future from tombs,
with spells force an empty mouth to speak.
The puppet corpse returning moves
reluctant to the necromancers' word;
he cannot let them know that living magic, how
the red king burning like a fox
has poured his blood into leaves and earth.

Yggdrasil

Withdrawn to his inner citadel
the Emperor can savour at leisure
this irregular season,
watching the swirling mist & leaves,
gyrations not prescribed by ritual.
Panegyric is replaced
by the stormy wood,
its voices through the boughs
calling on the death of richness.
No torches or musicians
divert his thought from this waning;
the night journey and bitter cold
trouble emperors with common fears.
And in the dark he can hear
one dry tree groan,
shuddering,
the Tree that props the world.

All Hallows

The black branch glistens,
weeping yellow leaves
along the watery night;

blood flows back into the ground,
trees' torches flare and die
in the last festival of fire.

The hollow wind strips all green,
leaving only ivy and the mortal yew;

in the stone a toad is alive,
silently preserving his jewel.

Some voice will survive this cold,
to celebrate the autumnless garden.

Merlin

Merlin sang the solstice' rod & rage,
dreaming of a prelapsarian garden
where branching sun confers
a stately clarity
on unfallen word that dances.

His incomplete mortality gives him clearer sight
into the rose or amethyst garden —
but we are of the destroying storm
that whirls us unrepentant through cloud
away from the ruined
paradise of language;

we glimpse its dream or ghost again
whenever man like Merlin sings.

Nature Note, March 1971

Flowers where no leaf yet stands
promise that eternal springtime
of heart and garden
that turning time
proves again a lie;

the pale bush
will not bear stars for fruit
this year, only berries,
and they will feed mere blackbirds,
not the phoenix from his heaven-tree.

Ars Longa

Alchemical fire burns through a shifting dapple of
    colours
to achieve its perfect ruby,
bringing forth golden work, a tree bearing suns.
In the mystical marriage of King and Queen,
ripening philosopher's gold in the heart,
we follow the soul on allegorical roads;
to seek & map the elixir or the poem,
we need the athanor, the devoted life, crystallising
power of Solomon's ring and throne.

ii

Within the fire's bright crystal
where Salamander blazes rosy white
lies our labyrinth's heart, the perfect Stone, in
cataract and spinning storm of gold.

Plain earth, or lead, or fallen man
the alchemist reforms into their single design,
bringing forth seeds of the sun
hidden deep in each dark body;

he disengages from every metal
that within it striving to become gold,
unearths & shows in clear strength
links of a buried unity; here poets learn

how to hold the burning-glass of words.

iii

Flamel sought through a treasury of images,
following power in purity, learning over decades
to pluck the mature gold
from its royal tree;
slowly the great colours wheel
out from death's night
through their peacock zodiac
to reach after patient years of fire
a glory that can turn the sea to Sun.

Abelard Solus

Natus est de virgine
sol de stella

Maria, bitter virgin,
diamond sea-star
hung in the chill wastes of air
above this gleaming level
where no sword will ever flash,
my harsh maidenhead cannot praise
your perfect state;
for I have known the solar fire
& burned in its heart
till I scorched my life and hers.
Although my red is turned to white now
in this desert of water and air,
despoiled by rebel & savage,
I stand in your silver light,
can have no worship for the freezing stars.
In a world now dead my songs for her
were sung through the morning town;
now in the pure Paraclete her nuns rehearse
my sterile theorems of God.
The sword has fallen truly
between us,
has divided me from what I was,
and there is no returning.

I cannot again be priest of that sun.

For Andrew

Streams that glitter through new grass
flow from a fountain winter sealed;
now rivers are loosed from the quiet cold
and feed on its bitter snow.

Perceiving a new thaw, poets warily
test bank & dyke, prepare to take the flood
& weave the clear net of channels
that will lead it through the fields.

Without them, waters pour down formless to the sea,
to the blank brightness of a sky,
a dazzle of infinitely moving waves,
to the shore that, opening, leads everywhere,
to exile that is everywhere the same.

The Third Way

We set out early, riding through the day
on the broad summer roads of Logres,
yet further out from Camelot
the paths grew narrower, & woodland nearer.
Approaching the borders of the other land,
one of us — or sometimes more — would start,
glimpsing some dream-creature among dim trees,
very close now; no more familiar wolf & boar,
but faun or centaur would appear for a moment,
then flick away into the undergrowth, leaving us
uneasily wondering whether to doubt
or to speak. It was difficult here to see birds,
and they seemed changed, and knowing.
We came with falling night
to the place where three ways meet,
the Road against Reason,
the Road without Mercy,
the Road without a Name.

And the third way brought us here,
to the Waste City;
demons that obeyed the enchanter Virgilius,
giants, or worse, must have built the nodding walls,

the vaulted palace and huge towers
whose ruin is our silent home;
we cannot read its inscriptions
or decipher its mosaics;
the images of Emperor & City are distorted
as by a witch's mirror or pack of cards;
we find no living soul here
but ourselves, who cannot leave.

Within the great night of magic . . .

Within the great night of magic
wizards move gracefully, sure-footed; can tell
from its pattern
where the diamond glass will crack,
what words infallibly attract
the queenly devil to dance or bed,
what planetary fire streams down
informing talisman or crystal at its hour.

The false magician's bartered self
must run the labyrinth's gauntlet, whirling
deeper to its core, unable
to pause, to will a moment's rest.
At every turn there hurtles up to meet him
a painted, fairground Queen of Cards;
shifting shapes that mock his desperation
hunt him ever down   to the silence where
his own scorched image stands before
a weary mirror webbed with scars.

To the Queen at Nonsuch

addressed to Elizabeth I in the late 1590s

' — The city in your dream (not the one
your imperial builders are already sketching)
is an ivory carving, or a jewel
from your regalia, of pearl
and crystal and amethyst, or an illumination
against a flat gold sky from a Book of Hours,

but outside your wall are rings of land
under the grey sea-mist
where witches christen cats and raise the storm
to kill a king,
where servant-girls dance for the Devil
and a farmer's wife shifts her shape to cat or hare
till she come home again; there

is no precision of detail, no delight in elaboration
of beauty —
ugliness of word and action
matches the intent.

The witch that cripples and blasts may appear
as only a mocking obverse to your dream;
but your brocaded ritual may become
self-absorbed as her jagged turning,
may hypnotise and strangle —
beware your obedient creation, and take care
that it be true.'

At South Leigh

In the supernatural wind
that whirls his white cloak, ruffling
great gold wings —
the fierce angel of sword and balance.

Beyond him gape the jaws
of darkness' old dragon,
and above like sparks in smoke
teeter crooked flying horrors.

Untouched by the gales that thrill his feathers
Our Lady stands above her silver moon,
star-crowned and wearing the small sun,
prays for the shivering soul.

The doctrines of courtesy interweave
all creatures in replacement, intercession;
the picture speaks of a lost certainty
to those now who have to unriddle it.

For a Wilderness

Out on the rim of the dark
roam outlaw, Fian, hermit,
who reject your ceremonies
of peacock & pomegranate city,
order and the vine.

Hervör walked among the mounds,
where graves opened all around her
blazing and roaring —
only there in a space between worlds
might she find the dead man's treasure.

Along the lonely edge of waters
Orpheus idly scribbles with a stick
on the sand;
far off a pale sea glitters
& day's waves close over his head.

In solitude the work is ripened,
achieves the blessing.

Lyric

When shall my spring come
and the singing voice   again
praise your rich beauty,
calm delights;

will you hear kindly
such unskilful song,   favour
poor lovers dazed by
your pleasures,

driven to dreaming?
You walk as the sun   that draws
the small clouds after
its shining;

they follow the fire,
bewildered by that   strong love,
know they throng to their
destruction.

Dr Dee Alone

To recall the dead, he says,
is not difficult,
force the tongueless mouth to tell
where treasures lie;
the crumbling figure stammers out its knowledge
beyond our circle's boundary.

By talisman, words of power I teach him,
are bound elemental & daemon
invisible to me;
I dare to unclasp the book
& trace the pentacle, but gaze in vain
into his darkened glass.

Through my learning he might command
that Lucifer, lord of ruined kingdoms;
he might achieve our Elixir,
to re-create (or is it to preserve?)
in Medea's cauldron of memory
the old and dying body.
The immortal mind in that prison cries,

God's mercy let me *see* what I believe and know!

Mosaics

Here our strange madness
begins to find out
the shape dozing in the rock,
patterns of the green holly;
within this point of making, root of dreams,
lie coiled all our possible creatures,
content to be nothing
until the light calls,
since able to be any thing,
able to fly or fall.

Before the roaring trees marched over it
smashing the mosaics' geometry, here stood
a discipline of marble and gold,
printed out its pattern of severe beauty
to fend off anarchy and the biding wood.

Store away carefully the tesserae, coloured and blank,
for one ignored may be the key
of that final design, still unknown;
patiently wait for the crystallising word
to strike jewels from the stone.

Time and the Hour

We returned, expecting the faithful place
to have waited unchanged
in the rays of its long afternoon;
we half-remembered, half-invented, details
of brambles, or a crooked branch,
or yellow apples in long grass; we said,
'That hedge will still be the same'
(forgetting we could now see over it);
'no-one here could fell a tree
or efface a line our memories know.'

Perhaps it was the wrong time of year,
or we had grown estranged;
a cloud-heavy sky rushed upon us, covering
all colour and the unfamiliar shapes.

King Priam is dead with his city
and his lasting monument.

Saturn drags his cold club-footed way . . .

Saturn drags his cold club-footed way
over memory, pattern he breaks, fouls
& scores with leaden furrow;
relics of belief must crumble
at his damp & ragged breath,
tower and altar splinter
before the invading fig-tree's root.

Lamentation for great Pan
faded long ago above a calm,
star-teeming sea,
and the women's voices mourning Adonis
drift into indifferent quiet;
in one place alone they remain,
this luminous abiding city of the mind.

Of Mutability

Here branching bone and the constant rock
are wrought by the waves
into shapes they bear   within eternity's mirror,
regain their inward self, after long wandering.

The island in time's river-ring
is worn thin as the shoulder-blade of a hare
for wizards' divination,
thin as the finger-nail moon.

A bonfire's ashes
glint with shards of glass
grey & silver in the white sun;
great Babylon is a mound of copper dust.

All forms flow down to that one sea
whose rich depth enfolds them,
travel their interlacing roads
to the primal wood, the mid-land-ocean,

where all names rest   in their beginning,
out of the light of sun and moon,
where even Time will come at last
when his day is ended.

One of the lost Grail Knights speaks

As rutting summer wearies, and the night
begins to climb stealthily nearer,
the regal sun is travelling down
to scarlet sacrifice;
here sleepy, monstrous-coloured fruits
foam from the branches, or rot in purple shadow —
this is the devilish garden.
Idle, intolerable over-ripeness
lies all around me
these yawning, sultry days,
but even here the bright pain
returns, and I must remember. . .

Once, long ago, I believed
in the Quest; desired that lofty palace
in a land between heaven and earth
transmuting what was mortal.

But I could not breathe its air, I said, nor make
myself worthy; rejecting its grace, I turned away
to choose this poisoned, lying summer.
I dared not take the silent road
past Chronos' tower to the Fortunate Isles.

Sauros

for Paul

Huge beast heaves down through grey saltings to grey
    sea
as day crawls over a leafless land;
there are no birds yet.
A round horizon's edge cuts down
as water receives him, daylight's hunter.

When his kind has vanished far
into earth's forgetting ages,
he will be Leviathan, king of howling Ocean
who can snap the world in his tightening coils,
power of secret waters & hollows under the earth,

unfathomable, darkness,
who chills our deepest dream.

Astrologer

When autumn's fever half-awakens ancient memories,
when dreams uncoil from their cave in broad daylight
to mingle with its creatures & to cloud the sun,
he climbs again the intricate narrow stair
to his tower room, and follows
Time's journeying, the curving road of stars,

makes ready to cross great Oceanus river
whose waves encircle our tiny world,
to sail beyond the pillars of the sun.

He leaves each familiar boundary,
moves easily through night's hollow vastness
towards ever-retreating Thule,
the pure Hesperides,
or Siren islands white-ringed with bones.

Leaving Troy

Sown with salt, black furrows mark
a dead place where no seed can grow,
grave of our immortal, god-guarded city.

Dragons couch in pride's palace now,
their scales grate & clang on gold
sceptre & jewel tarnishing into earth.

For a few years more we can keep alive
an empty name that stands for nothing here,
until our final exile comes.

My voice blows down the miles of night,
lost among the chill slate colonnades.

Titania

She twirls a blue rose, idly
cracks each bud with her nail
to find its cut heart shrivelled
black by frost; around her
a serene & scented air denies
all snow & ashes of the winter heart,
brittle branch or stream, the falling tower —
these lie outside her proud magic,
warped into painted shadow
by its radiance.

Must my twilight remain that crystal's foil,
is it only fool's gold, Lady, that I bring?

In a twilight between two stars . . .

In a twilight between two stars
your quiet beauty wanders,
among dark streams and broad-winged trees
that stir their feathers in a gentle air;

you listen to shadow's voice here
& the sigh of hidden birds,
when a cold mad moon dances
over green gloom.

Through racing stillness of the sky
her influence thrills down,
marks you out her own
with print of silver seal,

ripens treasure in veins that are
the galleries of her mines.

By this Light

The moon is blazoned in her plenitude
and makes the air with brightness tremble;
empty-handed, all beauty stands in her shadow.

High wisdom in a mist of radiance
is obverse of aphasiac folly
cackling miserly over hoarded husks.

'Wherever in the two worlds you may be
you will find no place empty of my light;
follow my shining myth of lunacy.'

Out from havens of the sun, Domina,
king, fool & poet sail each autumn
for the hidden island of your promise.

Cormac Looks at the Crucifix

Crom Cruach was an idol
axes hacked from bog-oak
black as a toad,
a golden mask on his face
& twelve gods squatting round him.
We gave them blood sacrifice
before the white power came,
with bell and crook and shaven head,
prophesied by druids;
at Patrick's command foul creatures
came swarming out of our gods,
mice and blow-flies, lumps of carrion
scurried, and vanished.

Crom Cruach bowed his hams and died,
falling before the rootless living tree.

Where grass-green starlight falls . . .

Where grass-green starlight falls
upon a winter country,
you can see them, in the distance,
moving, three or four, along the bank
of pallid marsh or corrupted lake,
shapes that drift in a fretful wind,
mere folds in air that trouble sight,
no sound or gesture permitted them
save that swaying in mummified air.

I must travel the land of their despair
a long familiar time.

Wait, learning patience . . .

Wait, learning patience; learn clarity, observing;
admit no forgery; await harsh night
when, most incredible, the word strikes true,
unsought, except through all the labyrinth,
to shock the heart into a strong delight
— to love, a private joy where lies no rest.

Woodchester

Step into this charmed reach
                    if you dare;
here Orpheus turns a globe
                    of translucent air
strangely solid like ice

where all beasts fall gentle,
                    stand at gaze;
fox with peacock, partridge,
                    gryphon, thread his maze,
feel no hate or hunger.

Orpheus butchered, headless,
                    evermore
sings to sea and mountain,
                    within the wind's core
inhabiting stillness.

Electra

'In my dream I stood in a grey land
that had never known tree or sun,
and a little crooked wind blew from nowhere
fretting my hair;
under tarnished heavy clouds
distance or direction were impossible,
no choice could hold meaning.

It was like the salt marshes that creation's gale
streams across in the blackness before day,
but here there was no sea,
here there could be no dawn.

And I slowly remembered fragments
of a life unimaginably distant,
of a child's past, in clefts of time's canyon
freakishly revealed —
my green dress, my toys and games,
all my broken morning.

This is everyman's unknown home, they murmured,
end of journey for stylite and conquistador —
alone before a tomb in a faceless land.'

And all this eternal while Orestes avenger
is hastening down great roads to return to that tomb.

This autumn weather . . .

This autumn weather smokily
         mocks our eyes —
the great leaden bubble of a dome
         flattens into silhouette,
Jack Shadow changes tree to man,
         or casual face to lost familiar,
for a long moment
         of welcome treachery,

wakens into clarity another eye
         that scries truer images
beyond the prisoning cave.

Notes

Ars Longa (page 18): Flamel was a fourteenth-century Parisian scribe and bookseller who turned alchemist in his old age and achieved the Magnum Opus.

At South Leigh (page 26) : The church of South Leigh in Oxfordshire has a wall-painting of St Michael weighing a soul; on one side devils try to pull it down, and on the other Our Lady stands, representing the Doctrine of Exchange or Substitution, the co-inherence of all souls whereby they contribute to each other's salvation (*Arthurian Torso*, pp. 123, 143), and the Atonement.

For a Wilderness (page 27): The warrior Angatýr's sword was buried with him, and the only person who could retrieve it was his daughter Hervör (it had to be a man's son usually, but Angatýr had no sons); she succeeded, in spite of the attempts of the dead in the other burial-mounds to prevent her. Such magic swords would not go with any but the next closest representative of the family after their master's death.

Woodchester (page 44) : At Woodchester in Gloucestershire is a magnificent fourth-century mosaic pavement of Orpheus surrounded by beasts and birds, which is only uncovered about once in ten years, because it lies under the churchyard.

Dark of Day

Jack-in-the-Green solemnly revolves, jigging,
clothed in his nest, a diagram of boughs,
Hooden Horse claps his wooden jaws
as the fiddle unreels rhythmed monotony.

Beyond his figure the third eye sees
divine green kings move destined
along inflexible ritual, spilling their blood
to earth's renewal.

In my End is my Beginning,
for ever.